ADDITION BY ADOPTION

Kids, Causes & 140 Characters

Published by Monkey Outta Nowhere
Saint Paul, Minnesota

www.MonkeyOuttaNowhere.com
www.KevinDHendricks.com
Copyright © 2010 by Kevin D. Hendricks

Cover design by Brian White
Layout by Ronald Cox

ISBN: 1451581386
EAN-13: 978-1-4515-8138-6

Printed by CreateSpace in the United States of America

DEDICATION

To Lexi and Milo. You made this possible. I love you, always. No matter how many times you throw up on me.

And for the eventual day when you find this book so totally embarrassing: I'm sorry. Sorta. Just keeping picking dandelions and you'll be OK.

TABLE OF CONTENTS

INTRODUCTION

I'm a work-at-home dad. I sit at the kitchen table with a laptop, eating a bowl of cereal and telling my daughter no. I schedule conference calls during *Sesame Street*, because it's more predictable than naptime. I recycle office paper twice, not because I'm a treehugger, but because the backside of expense reports is the perfect canvas for a 3-year-old.

I have two kids, two dogs and half a dozen clients at any one time. We're a one-car family, which my wife drives to work every day before the sun comes up. My life is a constant juggling act. But that's OK, I spent a summer as a yo-yoing street performer—it wasn't juggling, but it wasn't easy either.

I'm not one of those parents who thinks children are a blessing. They may be a blessing, but they're also a curse. Talk to me about blessing when you're cleaning puke out of a kid's hair in a truck stop restroom somewhere in Missouri and she's screaming because the toilet flushes too loud. Parenting is tough. Sometimes I long for a cush job, like bodyguard, stunt double or president of the United States. Something with no pressure.

Parenting is also amazing. Like when your 10-month-old finally stops screaming and you can just sit in the rocking chair and be exhausted together. Or when your 2-and-a-half-year-old points out the window and says, "Look Daddy, a mural!" and you realize she's been listening all along.

In June of 2007 I started posting on the micro-blogging site Twitter, a social media site that asks you the question "What are you doing?" and limits your response to 140 characters. Anything that could be accomplished in the moment between me saying no and the resulting temper tantrum was worth checking out.

In June of 2007 I also stopped using Twitter. Like everybody else who tries it, I didn't get it.

But six months later in December of 2007 I tried again. Answering that little question, "What are you doing?", was intriguing. It turns out nobody cares what you're doing right now (the literal answer would always be posting to Twitter, and so in 2009 Twitter updated the question to the more colloquial, "What's happening?"), but that 140-character limitation opens up the doors to creative freedom.

Nobody cares that I'm eating breakfast, but it turns out some people at least think it's funny that I have not one but two distinct songs about breakfast time. Nobody cares that I'm watching NASCAR, but people do care that my daughter confuses NASCAR with one of her favorite movies, "Mada-Mada-Mascar" (*Madagascar*). Nobody cares that I'm sitting on the couch, but they do care when I collapse on the couch with snacks and TV in order to restore sanity.

It turns out tweeting (the verb for posting to Twitter) about my life as a work-at-home dad is somewhat interesting. So I started tweeting the goofy things my daughter said, the bizarre arguments we get into, and the curious and wonderful things that children do.

After a while I realized these 140-character snapshots of parenting might be something. Random friends and even strangers would comment about the latest thing Lexi said. At the very least they were the kind of something my grandma would love to read. But surprise, surprise, she doesn't use Twitter. So I started collecting these parenting tweets into the book you now hold in your hands.

But something else interesting happened along the way. I realized that in between the tweets about my taco man song and potty training gone awry, there were tweets about my son's adoption. Threaded between goofy comment and peculiar moment was the story of how my son came home. The entire process was in there, from expectant waiting, to traveling to Ethiopia to bring him home, to the daily milestones as he became a part of our family.

Then something even more interesting happened. Twitter went beyond a simple tool to report on change, and it became an agent of change itself. I turned 30 in June 2009 and decided to commemorate the milestone by raising enough money to provide 30 people with clean water. I offered to shave my head as an incentive, dubbed it the Bald Birthday Benefit and mercilessly flogged the effort on Twitter. I shaved my head on my 30th birthday and celebrated clean water for 130 people. It wouldn't have happened without Twitter as a tool to bang the drum for the organization charity: water.

Suddenly this was no longer a mere collection of tweets. It wasn't a Twitter book version of *Kids Say the Darndest Things* (besides, Bill Cosby has the loving-yet-still-mocking-your-kids market locked up) or just a glimpse of my family's adoption. Suddenly it offered a snapshot of something more.

Sometimes life is a surprise. A crazy, wonderful, try-not-to-swear-in-front-of-the-kids surprise. So I share this story with you. Parenting is hard. It's also hilarious. But it changes the world.

And for all the stress I endure day in and day out, my wife does it ten times over. She's a kindergarten teacher. Bless her heart.

(Yes, I can appreciate the irony of an 800-word introduction to a book full of 140-character riffs. Aren't you clever.)

Disclaimer

This book is a curated list of tweets about my daily life. Tweets have been specially selected and edited for context and clarity. Much of the technical Twitter-speak has been removed, including hashtags, @replies and abbreviations used to sneak under that 140-character limit. @, &, u, w/, and 4 might work in Twitter, but it's just ridiculous to read them in a printed book. In some cases these changes have pushed the character count beyond Twitter's ironclad 140-character limit. But we're not on Twitter anymore, are we? I've also tried to keep the tweets in chronological order, though it's possible they're not perfect. In summary, we're going for context and clarity over accuracy.

MEET THE FAMILY

A quick 140-character introduction to my family so the tweets that follow make a little more sense.

Kevin
That's me. I'm the not-so-patriarch, the introvert who would rather hide behind his computer than interact with people and often does.

Abby
My wife lets the kids make a mess and rolls with it. She studied child development and knows what she's doing. I'm just along for the ride.

Lexi
The spitfire and star of the show, Lexi is now 4 (going on 15). She wants you to know her birthday cake is in January.

Milo
The newest addition, Milo comes late in the game, but he gives the heart to this little tale. He says, "Thbbbtt!"

Speak
A Pekingese poodle mix named for The Tick's stalwart hound, he's tiny and grumpy, like an old man. He also does modeling. Seriously.

Mazie
She's a rat terrier-corgi mix full of self-esteem issues. Mazie's not sure if she should bark or run and hide, so she'll do both.

CHAPTER 1: WAITING

From a purely practical perspective adoption has always made perfect sense to me. There are so many children in this world who don't have loving families, why wouldn't you want to welcome one into your heart? I wanted to adopt because it seemed like the most loving, sensible and logical thing to do—which is kind of funny because parenting is rarely sensible or logical. But the compassion in my heart told me it was a no-brainer.

It also helped that Abby hated being pregnant.

Our adoption process officially began in August 2007. By Christmas we had turned in all our paperwork and were added to our agency's waiting list. And so it began.

We were adopting a boy or girl from Ethiopia under 12 months old. Our agency added us to a waiting list with hundreds of other eager parents to wait for our referral, adoption parlance for the moment we were matched with a child. Once you get a referral the child could be in your home in a matter of months. But until then you wait. And that's where our story begins.

We told Lexi all about the adoption process. She knew a baby sister or brother would be coming, but just like us she didn't know when. We talked endlessly about Ethiopia and soon Lexi could point out the country on a world map. We even posted a video of her saying Ethiopia—it sounded like "Yopi-opia."

One of the hardest realities is that somewhere during that waiting period our kid was born. One of those days when we were standing around in the empty baby's room or jumping when the phone rang—our kid was born into a situation that wasn't going to work out. For whatever reason some family was falling apart.

"Adoption is a last resort," said Haddush Haleform, head of the Children's Commission under Ethiopia's Ministry of Labor, as quoted in the heart-wrenching book *There Is No Me Without You*. "I am deeply respectful of the families who care for our children. But I am so very interested in any help that can be given to us to keep the children's parents alive in the first place. Adoption is good but children, naturally, would prefer not to see their parents die."

I think adoption is an incredible thing, but it doesn't fix the underlying problem.

This is part of why Ethiopia will always have a place in our hearts. As much as we love Milo, we want his brothers and sisters to be able to stay with their families in Ethiopia. In an ideal world adoption wouldn't be necessary. To anyone feeling like they can't adopt, there are so many things you can do to ensure that children don't need to be adopted.

As you can imagine, it's an emotional juggernaut. And all you can do is wait. Abby went to work. I stayed home with Lexi and worked in the evenings. We embraced other causes and the realities of Ethiopia began to have their subtle affect on us. Life continued to unfold around us, but through it all we were waiting, in eager anticipation for that child that was to come.

JANUARY **2008**

Dancing to the "Taco Man" song (my own take on the "Macho Man" song I sing while making tacos) because it makes Lexi laugh hysterically.
January 7, 2008

Watching Lexi and another 2-year-old turn the handicap ramp at Barnes & Noble into a playground.
January 9, 2008

Loving the surprised looks on Lexi's face when I burst into her room while she's supposed to be napping.
January 9, 2008

Trying to reconcile my faith and the staggering difference between my wealth and the incredible poverty throughout the world. Too heavy.
January 13, 2008

Trying to coordinate Lexi's naptime with a business conference call. This is a doomed endeavor.
January 15, 2008

Just got fingerprinted by Homeland Security for our adoption. They used wicked cool digital finger scanners. Sure beats the county's ink.
January 16, 2008

Taught Lexi the word 'pariah,' as in: "You'll be a pariah if you run around naked all day and refuse to put clothes on."
January 22, 2008

"Orphans won't be orphans forever." (Psalm 10:14, *The Message*)
January 24, 2008

Lexi just sent her stroller (with the baby) careening over the stairs. Note to self: Don't let Lexi push the new baby in the stroller.
January 29, 2008

FEBRUARY 2008

My 2-year-old is now a photographer. Go technology!
February 1, 2008

After a long, stressful day with Lexi I had to get out and unwind. Some people would drink. I went to the library. I'm such a bad ass.
February 9, 2008

Lexi just demanded that I tickle her, then informed me I wasn't doing it right: "No, no, no! Both hands!"
February 15, 2008

Lexi is praying in the bathtub: "Pray adopted baby amen." "Pray mama amen." "Dear God amen."
February 22, 2008

MARCH 2008

Lexi is singing "Taking care of the baby" to herself while she wraps her doll in a dishtowel.
March 5, 2008

Sometimes I think Lexi is the cheese version of Cookie Monster. "I'm eating cheese! Ahm, ahm, ahm..." (No seriously, she just said that!)
March 14, 2008

Not only did Lexi have to bring her teddy bear, Pinky, to church today, but Pinky had to go up for communion.
March 16, 2008

Just made a snowman with Lexi. Well, I made a snowman, she sort of helped and mostly walked up and down the front steps.
March 18, 2008

So Lexi likes to pick her toe jam. Seriously. This morning she was actually singing a song about it: "Toe jam, toe jam, toe jam!" with actions!
March 21, 2008

My daughter just called me downstairs to look at her "soup-soup" (swimsuit), then pushed me back upstairs.
March 22, 2008

Pinky, my daughter's teddy bear, is currently sitting on the potty chair. God speed, Pinky.
March 24, 2008

When the first thing your daughter says in the morning is "I throwed up," you know it's going to be a fun day.
March 25, 2008

APRIL 2008

Lexi just told Abby to go sit in the corner.
April 1, 2008

Reading about food riots in poor countries while eating my second bowl of cereal and throwing Lexi's soggy Cheerios away. That's unsettling.
April 15, 2008

Me: "Lexi, you've single-handedly raised the volume level in our household." Lexi: "NOOOOOOOOOO!"
April 16, 2008

Going through Pepsi withdrawal. Trying to remember little children through out the world without Pepsi. If they can do it, I can do it for a day.
April 18, 2008

Lexi is obsessed with W's. She just spotted one on the back of a magazine and tried to tickle it. "Tickle W! Tickle W!"
April 24, 2008

Eating breakfast with Lexi and my nephew Ari. I keep calling him "Buddy." Sheesh, I'm the guy who calls little kids 'buddy.'
April 28, 2008

MAY 2008

Taking Lexi swimming tonight. I don't look forward to these type of things like I should (too much work?), but they always end up being fun.
May 1, 2008

Vet diagnosed Speak (my dog) with a "traumatic sports injury." He did the 3-mile walk for the Humane Society on Saturday and slipped his kneecap.
May 8, 2008

Taking Mazie to the vet. God help us all.
May 12, 2008

Wow, Mazie didn't scream at the vet. She peed on the floor when a much bigger dog sniffed her butt, but who hasn't done that?
May 12, 2008

Lexi has three kinds of cereal for breakfast: Cheerios, Fruity Cheerios and Wheaties—all mixed together. I've created a monster.
May 14, 2008

Up to #35 on the unofficial adoption waiting list. Folks much higher on the list have gotten referrals, so the phone could ring any day.
May 28, 2009

We're #30 on the unofficial adoption waiting list. Last night I dreamed they called and left a message and I couldn't make out the phone number to call back.
May 30, 2009

After trying to attach a diaper to her doll's head, Lexi is now trying to diaper her own foot. Note to self: Keep new baby away from Lexi.
May 30, 2008

We're looking for something fun to do on a Friday night with a 2-year-old. Currently debating the definition of "fun."
May 30, 2008

JUNE 2008

Lexi is enjoying four kinds of cereal. It'd be six, but I refuse to open more and Cinna-Bunnies aren't a hit. Variety is the spice of wastefulness.
June 3, 2008

Lexi congratulated me for opening the door to her room this morning: "Yay! You did it!" (claps hands). I'm being patronized by a 2-year-old.
June 5, 2008

During lunch Lexi handed me her spoon and said it was a call from Mommy. A spoon phone. I wonder if Maxwell Smart knows about her.
June 5, 2008

I like to get Lexi to try saying funny words like guacamole and lanyard. Parenting may have its challenges, but there are upsides.
June 9, 2008

I just realized the similarities between my daughter and Twitter. Both are always asking, "What are you doing?"
June 10, 2008

Wife and kiddo are off to gymnastics ("gym-snastics") this morning. Let's see if I can actually be productive this morning. Doubtful. Very doubtful.
June 19, 2008

Lexi shouts up the stairs: "Daddy, it's time for hungry!" I think I need to go eat lunch.

June 19, 2008

JULY 2008

Awoke to sound of 2-year-old saying she had poop in her bed, but it was just attention seeking lies.

July 1, 2008

My daughter has climbed into the dog kennel, on her own mind you. Things are never dull around here.

July 1, 2008

The tag in Lexi's shorts says "Keep Away From Fire." That's some good parenting advice.

July 1, 2008

We just had a Lexi-cane. Or maybe a Lexi-nado. At any rate, it was panic and craziness in her wake. Now it's kisses for all and bedtime.

July 8, 2008

Gearing up for a day at the zoo with our monkey—I mean Lexi.

July 8, 2008

I just told Lexi that orange juice is not a toy.

July 10, 2008

While bathing Lexi figures out how to look up so water poured on her head doesn't go in her face: "I got it, I got it, I got it, I got it!"

July 11, 2008

My dog Mazie: "Oh my gosh, rabbit in the yard, rabbit in the yard! I'msoexcitedther ewasarabbitintheyardtoday—oops, forgot to pee outside."

July 14, 2008

Lexi has misplaced her pants.
July 17, 2008

I've just decided that Lexi isn't 2-and-a-half, she's 2-and-a-spazz.
July 22, 2008

Lexi just proudly showed me the poop in her potty chair. High fives all the way around. Though I won't photograph this particular milestone.
July 24, 2008

Overheard wife to daughter on the way to VBS: "You have to share Jesus... you don't get to hold Jesus all the time."
July 30, 2008

AUGUST **2008**

Abby: "You can have one or zero band aids (not two)." Lexi: "Zero!" (Clearly, we're not understanding the concept of zero)
August 3, 2008

Tonight I kept singing "Lexi, Lexi" to the tune of "Lovefool" ("Love me, love me / Say that you love me") by the Cardigans, and Lexi was quickly imitating me. Hilarious.
August 3, 2008

Abby and Lexi rode the bus on Monday and on the way home Lexi said: "Dear God, thank you for the city bus. Amen." Best prayer ever.
August 6, 2008

Me: "Lexi, are you a spazzasaurus?" Lexi: "...duck! because I love my duck! [pause] Yes. [pause] Because I love my duck! Because I love my..."
August 7, 2008

As much as I love hearing Lexi sing "Waves of Mercy" over the baby monitor, I am not letting her get away with a one hour nap. No way.
August 11, 2008

Unforeseen brand issues: Told Lexi about my company, Monkey Outta Nowhere, and she pronounced it "Monkey on New Butter" and "Monkey Underwear."
August 15, 2008

First full day of back to school (i.e, back to full time daddy daycare) and I'm remembering how hard it is to be productive in the afternoon.
August 18, 2009

Our dog Speak got a haircut yesterday and now it seems he's a rock star. Lexi pushed Mazie (our other dog) away and called for Speak.
August 26, 2008

The 'You can be what you want to be' moment in the Hilary Clinton video at the Democratic National Convention made me teary eyed as a dad of a daughter and soon a black child. And I don't like Hilary.
August 27, 2008

Lexi: "I'M NOT CRABBY!" Sure kid, whatever you say.
August 27, 2008

Strange things Lexi said: "Butter in the pasta? That's not safe."
August 29, 2008

Told Lexi that whoever wins the election in November, history will be made. She responded, with a total inflection at the end: "History made?"
August 29, 2008

Lexi: "Eating a strawberry? That's not safe."
August 29, 2008

Yesterday I told Lexi she could read one book before naptime. She picked the 250-page *Sesame Street Dictionary*. Kids are sneaky.
August 29, 2008

SEPTEMBER *2008*

Our adoption agency just sent out an e-mail telling people the wait time is up to 12 months. Bah. That would put us at Christmas. Humbug.
September 5, 2008

- -

Things I never thought I'd hear myself say: "I can go outside because I have pants on."
September 8, 2008

- -

Watched Lexi play air guitar during the youth group's worship set tonight. I'm so proud.
September 11, 2008

- -

Lexi's lunch: Peanut butter sandwich (no jelly), carrots, apples, yogurt, cheese stick. I don't know where she gets her eating habits, but it's not from me.
September 11, 2008

- -

Lexi spent some time this afternoon jumping up and down on her bed singing worship songs while naked. Weird, but biblical.
September 14, 2008

- -

Lexi refuses to use the toilet, but she has started changing her own pull-up. I'm not sure if this is progress or not.
September 14, 2008

- -

45 minutes after skinning her knees, Lexi starts crying. I have no idea when that happened. Apparently she didn't either.
September 15, 2008

- -

Lexi upon waking up this morning: "I've got crusties in my nose!"
September 16, 2008

- -

Watched an obnoxious kid fall into the animatronic alligator display at Rainforest Cafe and get soaked. I enjoyed it a little too much.
September 21, 2008

- -

I'm going to be homeless on Oct. 16. Sleeping out to raise money and awareness for homelessness. Wanna support me?

September 25, 2009

OK, the Mercedes Benz C300 ad from Google that was showing up on my blog post, "I'm Going to Be Homeless"? Ironic. (It's gone now.)

September 25, 2009

I won't be homeless until Oct. 16. At least that's when I *plan* on being homeless—but you don't really plan that, do you?

September 29, 2009

OCTOBER 2008

Lexi woke up at 2 a.m., got out of bed and made a mess of her room. Sigh. Fuel for the 'toys in one room, sleep in other room' idea.

October 4, 2008

According to Lexi, it's not junk mail, it's "jumping mail." Which you have to admit sounds a lot more interesting.

October 5, 2008

We're up to #16 on the unofficial adoption waiting list. Woot, woot! It's encouraging to finally see some movement after months of nothing.

October 7, 2009

If Lexi asks 'why' one more time I think my head is going to explode. They do stop being 2-year-olds eventually, right?

October 7, 2008

T-minus one week until I'm homeless (for a night). Any more takers on supporting emergency shelters in the Twin Cities?

October 8, 2009

Everybody needs an intern. And my daughter keep scribbling on everything with a sharpie. She's out.
October 9, 2008

Up to #14 on unofficial adoption waiting list. Excited, but trying not to get too excited. Phone rang today and made me wonder, is this it? No.
October 9, 2008

Abby: "Purple monkey dishwasher." (what we say whenever we can't understand Lexi's mushmouth) Lexi: "There's no monkeys in the dishwasher."
October 12, 2008

Oh, we're up to #11 on the unofficial adoption list. Woot, woot.
October 13, 2008

Lexi: "Mazie (our dog) is probably upstairs. I'm going to go to talk to her. See what's going on."
October 13, 2008

I'm homeless tonight. Current temp: 37. On the plus side, tonight's overnight low looks to be only 42. Yay?
October 16, 2009

Just suited up for my night of homelessness. Trying to pack minimally, but smartly. Low of 42 overnight: Think warm thoughts, boy.
October 16, 2009

I draw the line at doing the Macarena to stay warm.
October 16, 2009

Time for bed. Thinking about the many homeless families out there. G'night.
October 16, 2009

Survived the night. Barely. Homelessness sucks.
October 17, 2009

So my homeless experience? Awful. OK, so being sick wasn't part of the plan, but I don't think the homeless have that choice.
October 18, 2009

Lexi is singing to her stuffed animals: "God answers pray, God answers pray ... He's so good to me. God love and so ... He's so good to me."
October 20, 2008

Told Lexi about a girl's hockey game I saw at the library (they moved the library to the Eagan Civic Arena during construction) and now she wants to play. That's my girl.
October 27, 2008

NOVEMBER 2008

Me: "I have to go get some work upstairs, I'll be right back." Lexi: "Daddy, you can't just go to work like that."
November 1, 2008

One million refugees flee fighting in the Democratic Republic of the Congo. Why is Africa always going up in flames?
November 2, 2008

Lexi is running around in circles in my office until she falls over. Then she gets up and does it again.
November 3, 2008

Today Lexi is running circles around the dog until she falls over. Then she gets up and does it again.
November 4, 2008

Lexi and I just voted. No waiting. Poll workers said the morning was very busy. Lexi: "Let's do it again!" Go democracy!
November 4, 2008

Why am I such a sap lately? Stories of first time voters, Obama's speech, dancing in the streets, kid hugging orphan—all make me want to cry.
November 6, 2008

Me: "Stop licking me! Why are you licking everything?!" Lexi: "Because I'm silly!"
November 10, 2008

For those clamoring for daughter updates, Lexi is asking for [pretend] coffee in a New England accent (cawfee!). Thanks Grandmas.
November 11, 2008

You want good news? OK, how about a family of six moving to Uganda for a year to finalize their son's adoption? That rocks.
November 13, 2009

More good news: Telling the stories of the homeless so they're no longer invisible: InvisiblePeople.tv
November 13, 2008

Social worker called—no referral for us, but a bunch of other eager families will get one. Yay for them, but more waiting for our adopted kiddo.
November 13, 2008

"Lexi, you're the next contestant on Pick a Bagel! Come on down!" [Cue music, Lexi gets up and dances over to pick a bagel.] I'm such a dork.
November 15, 2008

Note to self: When dropping dogs off, don't bring the kid along if you can at all help it. She cried the whole way home.
November 21, 2008

CHAPTER 2: BOY

The call came while Abby was at school, in the bathroom of all places. Our 12 months of waiting finally ended. It was a boy.

We imagined that call coming so many times. Abby watched the unofficial waiting list daily, announcing and celebrating each and every move up the list. I preferred not to be reminded. But by the end we were both expectant and giddy, jumping any time the phone rang and then answering in disappointment.

Abby called me, breathless, giving details I could barely process. I rushed into the next room to tell Lexi she was a big sister. She frowned and didn't look away from the TV. Too engrossed in *Sesame Street*, she'd be excited later.

All the nebulous waiting suddenly had a picture, a child, a connection—and an end in sight. There were many hurdles to go, but we were almost there. The news came just after Thanksgiving and before Christmas, like Advent. Our Christmas card that year featured a picture of Lexi holding a picture of Milo.

Abby and I always struggled with the materialistic aspects of Christmas and this year we opted to do something different. Half the money we normally spent on gifts would be donated to the cause of our choice. So instead of spending $50 on Lexi, she'd get $25 in gifts and then $25 to donate. It was our new Christmas tradition, partly inspired by Abby's grandfather who had passed away just before Thanksgiving.

That year Abby gave all of her Christmas money to charity: water, an organization that provides clean water to people who don't have it. A fellow adoptive parent pushed people to give water for Christmas, and as Abby shared the stories and statistics I began to listen. Who could argue with water for Christmas? Lexi wanted to donate her Christmas money to Ethiopia, so we picked several causes that supported orphans, like her brother, in Ethiopia.

That winter had a profound sense of anticipation. Our family had been in limbo for a year, waiting and waiting. Now our family was separated and we longed to be together. We could only count the days and pray for our little one so far away. And life went on. There was Christmas, Lexi's birthday (which came with an ultimatum: no more diapers when you turn 3), a historic presidential inauguration and the coming hope of spring.

DECEMBER 2008

"I wanna hang up another Christmas tree!" -Almost 3-year-old Lexi, after we finished putting up the tree.
December 2, 2008

We got the call today. We're bringing home a baby boy from Ethiopia! He's 5 weeks old and so cute. We can go get him in two to four months. Woooooo!
December 3, 2008

Many, many thanks to everyone who has offered their congrats on our adoption news.
December 3, 2008

Lexi: "Daddy, what do you want for Christmas?" And then, in a very serious voice: "Do you want a green present?"
December 5, 2008

What do I want for Christmas? We got our little boy, so I'm set—though can't wait until he's home! But more orphans need homes: Consider adoption.
December 5, 2008

Up at 3 and 4 a.m. because Lexi's arms fell asleep and she woke up crying, telling her arm to "Wake up! Wake up!"
December 7, 2008

Doorbell rings. Lexi: "My baby brother Baby Sister is here!" (she's named her brother "Baby Sister" just like her dolls). Runs for the door.
December 8, 2008

Lexi went potty on the toilet today and there was much rejoicing. Best motivator? Ballpit at IKEA that requires children to be potty trained.
December 11, 2008

Lexi: "That dog's dancing on the piano! That's crazy." Can you guess what glimpse of a classic holiday special Lexi just saw?
December 11, 2008

Downside of wedding: Lexi wouldn't dance with me or let me dance with wife. Haven't felt that rejected since middle school.

December 13, 2008

Me: "Lexi, what do you want to get Momma for Christmas?" Lexi: "Kiss for Christmas!"

December 19, 2008

We got our adoption court date today: Feb. 20, 2009. Successful day in court means birth certificate, which gets us a travel date. Woo!

December 22, 2008

JANUARY 2009

They had ice skating school on *Sesame Street* today. Lexi wants to go so she can learn to skate so she can play hockey. Sweet.

January 1, 2009

Lexi got new Wall-E toothpaste and a Cookie Monster toothbrush (isn't that mixing genres?)—she's very excited. "Can I brush my teeth?!"

January 4, 2009

Lexi is in bed saying she wants to go to cowboy camp. That and checking her foot for 'ANDY' means a little too much *Toy Story.*

January 5, 2009

Lexi woke up coughing and then threw up. It's going to be one of those days. But now she's happily watching TV. Hmm... conspiracy?

January 6, 2009

Confession: I have *two* distinct Breakfast Time songs. Confession #2: I came up with them *before* I had kids.

January 6, 2009

Made a deal with Lexi: Try using the toilet for five minutes and you can watch a 45-minute Veggie Tales movie. I think I got taken for a ride.
January 7, 2009

Lexi is playing the role of birth control very well tonight.
January 12, 2009

Must summon all my super dad strength: Tonight I'm taking two almost-3-year-olds to *Sesame Street Live* by myself. I'm a hero or an idiot.
January 17, 2009

Survived *Sesame Street Live* with two almost-3-year-olds. Though I could go to bed now and it's only 9 p.m.
January 18, 2009

Me: "Lexi, today is the inauguration." Lexi: "Yay!" Me: "Do you know who's going to be president today?" Lexi: "Me, me, me!"
January 20, 2009

My kid must really love breakfast time. She just had a complete meltdown because we only have two cereals instead of the usual three.
January 21, 2009

Lexi: "I want something else to eat." Me: "We might have some peppers." Lexi: "Peppers? Woo peppers! I want peppers!"
January 21, 2009

Me: "OK, Lexi, five more minutes and it's going to be naptime." Lexi: "No! Two more minutes!" Me: "Er... OK."
January 22, 2009

Lexi just walked off dragging a yo-yo behind her. I'm so proud. Wait, she just came back with a slide whistle. Scratch that.
January 23, 2009

Lexi is cramming her baby doll in an empty peanut butter jar and putting on the lid. Uh... creepy?

January 23, 2009

- -

Lexi requested a 'W' cake for her birthday party today. It's her favorite letter. Perhaps thanks to the They Might Be Giants' song "Here Comes W..."

January 24, 2009

- -

Three-year-old Lexi: [looks down at the laptop] "Can I check my e-mail?"

January 25, 2009

- -

Having 5,000+ pics of your kid is great until you make a photo book and have to pick a finite number of photos. Doh. And she's only 3.

January 25, 2009

- -

Need a change of perspective? Babysit a 1- and 3-year-old plus your own 3-year-old when the 1-year-old refuses to be put down. We're dancing to U2 to stop a meltdown.

January 27, 2009

- -

Trying to talk my daughter into using the toilet is a complete waste. I'd pay her to use the toilet if it would work. But it won't.

January 29, 2009

- -

FEBRUARY 2009

My 3-year-old just went potty in the toilet. High fives all around!

February 2, 2009

- -

My kid just successfully used the toilet for the second time today! Feels silly to be so excited, but I'm tired of buying and changing diapers.

February 2, 2009

- -

Off to the store to get more bribery chocolate. The kiddo is using the toilet like a pro (or just working this whole bribery thing).

February 3, 2009

- -

Potty training continues in the Hendricks household. Today's lesson: The boy who cried wolf retold as the girl who cried poop.
February 4, 2009

Busy morning of potty training, which means productivity goes down there too.
February 4, 2009

My daughter just described her underwear as "wonderwear." An improvement, I think.
February 4, 2009

I love reading adoption stories. Brian Seay and his family just returned from Ethiopia with two kids this week. Go love!
February 6, 2009

Watching Lexi run in circles until she falls down, but I don't care because it's almost naptime and now she'll be more likely to sleep.
February 11, 2009

Lexi: "Daddy, can you get this sticker for me? My fingers are too sparkly." ?!
February 11, 2009

The Palmer family just moved to Uganda to finalize their adoption. Their new son Francis: "I have a family and they saved me!"
February 13, 2009

Lexi: "Look at me! I'm pretending to be a rice-er-onerous!" Ah, Saturday.
February 14, 2009

Not spending a dime on my wife for Valentine's Day and she loves me for it. This is how we've celebrated Valentine's Day since we got married.
February 14, 2009

Wise words from Lexi: "You don't take horses into the bathroom. Yuck."
February 16, 2009

Productivity is shot today. I blame everyone and everything but me.
February 17, 2009

Just listened to U2's "Get On Your Boots" and five minutes later Lexi is whispering it: "Let me hear the sound / Let me hear the sound..."
February 17, 2009

We just got our baby's social report. He's happy, peaceful and sleeps through the night! Love seeing the picture of him with a visible pic of us!
February 18, 2009

My day has been shot thanks to pics and updates about my kid in Ethiopia. I love it. Court day is Friday and if we get through then we can share.
February 18, 2009

Our adoption case goes to court in Ethiopia tomorrow. Pray that it goes smoothly. Thanks!
February 19, 2009

Thanks for the adoption prayers. Feels a bit selfish, so please pray for the many orphans out there: Love 'em, protect 'em, give 'em families.
February 19, 2009

Listening to U2's new album while waiting for word on our adoption. It's a good day.
February 20, 2009

Very thankful Lexi slept in this morning so I could hear U2's entire album in one sitting.
February 20. 2009

Lexi and I are listening to the new U2 over breakfast and we're both rocking out. Really liking "Magnificent" on second listen.
February 20. 2009

No adoption update yet (don't worry, you'll know). Trying to distract myself with new U2 and now *Lost*. Productivity=crap. Again.
February 20. 2009

We cleared court! Milo is officially ours and pics are going up now. Thanks for praying.
February 20, 2009

Say hello to Milo: Just posted a quick blog entry recapping the adoption news, what's next and processing the emotions.
February 20, 2009

Furiously posting updates about Milo to four different places, calling fam, e-mailing fam, etc. Oh and now an unexpected work call. Good but doh!
February 20, 2009

You know what's fun? Hanging out with a college guy 10 years younger than me who's not too cool to read my kid a bedtime story. Good day.
February 21, 2009

Don't want to shovel snow. Shoveling snow might wake up child who desperately needs a nap. Avoiding shoveling by blaming child. Score.
February 21, 2009

Can't say it enough, but many, many thanks to everyone who congratulated us on our adoption. Can't possibly respond to them all, so thanks.
February 24, 2009

More good adoption news: The six to eight week wait we were told (longer than we thought) was wrong. Four to six weeks: late March/early April. Woot, woot.
February 24, 2009

My dog ate a marker. A frickin' marker. How does that taste good? My other dog constantly pees on the carpet. This is last straw territory.
February 26, 2009

We're going to Ethiopia! Just got our travel dates: March 19. Woohoo!
February 26, 2009

- -

Lexi is making up for yesterday's subdued sickness with complete and total spazziness.
February 26, 2009

- -

Hard to believe that in T-minus 20 days we'll be leaving for Ethiopia and about to meet our son face to face. Woot, woot.
February 26, 2009

- -

My dog Mazie (yes, marker-eating dog) was just chewing on a matchbox car. Yeah, a diecast matchbox car. She dented the metal.
February 27, 2009

- -

Just booked flight to Ethiopia. Woot, woot. Rollercoaster emotions: excited about Milo, but some friends/family in crappy situations. Doh.
February 27, 2009

- -

While eating at Punch Pizza Lexi pretended to poke people with her fork, saying "Fork you! Fork you!" Except she doesn't pronounce her r's. Oops.
February 27, 2009

- -

Lexi: "I want to go see Jesus." Mom: "Where do you think he is?" Lexi: "Jesus is in Ethiopia!" Yes. Yes he is.
February 28, 2009

- -

CHAPTER 3: ETHIOPIA

March madness had never before been so fully realized. Nineteen months of work and waiting and expectancy came down to this: We left for the airport at 10:00 a.m. on Wednesday, March 18, 2009. Lexi would stay at home with her grandma, and Abby and I would fly to Ethiopia to meet Milo and bring him home. We'd never been away from Lexi for more than a day or two, let alone 10 days. I'd never traveled farther than Canada (Abby, the seasoned traveler, had been to England, El Salvador and deep into Mexico multiple times), but now we were going to cross an ocean for our son.

It's hard to put into words exactly what we felt in that moment. We were excited. Stressed. Giddy. Tired. Overjoyed. Busy.

It's amazing how the things of everyday life begin to fall away as you realize what's really important. Our to do list kept getting longer, but we kept hacking away at it. Some of my side projects were neglected. Other distractions were forgotten completely. I did manage to find time for certain stress-reducing diversions (preserving sanity is a priority). There's somehow always time for tickling, laughing or just sitting with Lexi. What needs to happen does, and the rest falls away.

Amid all the joyful stress of bringing Milo home, life still happened. Friends went through another miscarriage, a family crisis erupted, workplace drama escalated and the worldwide economic uncertainty was echoed in our bank account. Sometimes life is hard and messy and ugly, but there's always beauty. In that sense, I'm an insufferable optimist. Life may not always be happy, but it is joyful. For all the heartache and stress, it was also a jubilant time. A year and a half effort to expand our family was finally happening and no amount of stress or crisis could extinguish that joy.

I found myself crashing well after bedtime, throwing out reminders and questions to Abby until we both grew quiet and hopefully drifted off to sleep. In the quiet I found myself praying stream of consciousness prayers. They slipped in and out, finding and losing thoughts, rambling, like a child desperately trying to tell a parent everything on their mind and heart before they forgot. Like a child pleading for understanding, compassion, grace, rescue and comfort. I didn't know any other way. And I wouldn't have had it any other way.

I was going to meet my son.

We procured some very large suitcases today for our trip to Ethiopia. Lexi could very easily be a stowaway. We'll have to watch for that.
March 4, 2009

I was talking with Lexi about staying with Grandma while we go to Ethiopia. Lexi: "I want to go shopping with Grandma." They'll be fine.
March 5, 2009

Sh*t. Milo's been sick for a week in Ethiopia. Sounds like he's getting better now, but the little guy doesn't have much weight to lose.
March 6, 2009

International doctor says gastro problems are common. Hopefully Milo keeps getting better, but suck. Hate hearing this late and from afar.
March 6, 2009

My wife just pointed out that Lexi gave us a similar scare before she was born. Darn kids.
March 6, 2009

To cap off our wonderful day, Lexi threw up in the car on the way home. On the plus side, Lexi and Milo seem to be cross-continent bonding.
March 7, 2009

Lexi woke up at 6 a.m. and put the "Indescribable" song on repeat. Good news: She's still asleep. Bad news: Must kill Chris Tomlin. Must kill...
March 9, 2009

Me: "Did you just fart?" Lexi: "Yeah, cuz I want an orange." Me: [puzzled look]
March 9, 2009

Travel medical/evacuation insurance? Check. I love having friends with connections. Last year a friend had to be medivaced from Ethiopia. Worth $50.
March 9, 2009

Note to grandmothers: Lexi just told me there's too much stuff in her room to play.
March 9. 2009

Wondering if I should get a haircut before Ethiopia. Haven't had one since I shaved my head last June.
March 10, 2009

Just compiled directions/suggestions/how-to list for Lexi's grandma while we're gone: 22 pages. Yikes. Didn't mean to be so anal.
March 10, 2009

Thanks to a generous donation it looks like I will be tweeting from Ethiopia. Woot, woot!
March 10, 2009

Drive 10 miles to store. Kid throws up in car just before we get there. Drive 10 miles home. Didn't we play this game last week?
March 11, 2009

Trying to convince child she can't have toast mere minutes after throwing up. Ug. Can I be in Ethiopia now?
March 11, 2009

Lexi finally kept some food down. Ug, what a day. I'm exhausted. Hardly did any work, but did accomplish some packing. We leave in a week!
March 11, 2009

OK, the goal today is nobody throws up. That seems like a reasonable goal, right?
March 12, 2009

---

10 a.m. and no one has thrown up. That's worth a high five.
March 12, 2009

I'm pre-loading blog posts explaining what we'll be doing when in Ethiopia. I'm crying as I describe the day Milo comes into our care.
March 12, 2009

Apparently I'm nesting before Milo comes home. Male version of nesting? Moving furniture.

March 13, 2009

From Abby: My friend met her son today. Her son is Milo's roomie. Hearing her story makes me want to get on a plane to Ethiopia today.

March 13, 2009

Just got off the phone with a potential client whose mother used to work at our adoption agency. Love the connections. Go adoption!

March 13, 2009

One week from today I get to meet my son.

March 13, 2009

Just paid the credit card bill with the adoption travel expense in full and the bank didn't break. Should be last major expense. Thank you.

March 13, 2009

Two days before we leave. To do list is mostly done, just random, not-so-crucial stuff left. I'm feeling pretty scattered. Can we leave yet?

March 16, 2009

Prepping cameras for trip. 10 GB of storage, about 3,300 pictures. 330 pictures per day. That should be enough, right?

March 16, 2009

I am so beyond distracted this morning. What have I even been doing the last half hour? And Lexi isn't even up yet.

March 17, 2009

I think my VCR just died (yeah, we still have one of those) and Lexi almost missed *Sesame Street*. Better today when I can fix it, I guess.

March 17, 2009

One hour until our ride comes and the fun begins. Sadly, this will become a one-way conversation for the next 10 days. Sorry about that.
March 18, 2009

Big, big thank you to everyone for your comments, thoughts and prayers as we travel to Ethiopia to pick up Milo. We appreciate it so much.
March 18, 2009

Through security. Eating at TGI Friday's. Feel so international. Wait, no.
March 18, 2009

Lexi did good when we left. Smiles, hugs, no tears. A present helped. Bribery: Good.
March 18, 2009

On the plane to Ethiopia. Here we go.
March 19, 2009

Sorry for the lack of updates, text messages barred in Ethiopia. Tonight is the first time Internet has worked, so we'll update what we can.
March 20, 2009

We met our wide-eyed little boy today. He's very tiny and loves to watch everything going on. Quiet and cute. Made up for bewildering arrival.
March 20, 2009

Having never traveled farther than Canada before, I gotta say this trip is a bit overwhelming for me. But today with Milo made up for it.
March 20, 2009

Today we heard Milo squawk. Closest he's come to crying in the more than six hours we've spent with him so far.
March 21, 2009

Called Lexi today and she's doing great: "You flew on an airplane! Bye!" As we expected, she didn't care to talk much on the phone.
March 21, 2009

Emotional day in Southern Ethiopia meeting people important to Milo. Long trip (3.5 hours one way), but very worthwhile. Lots of joyful tears.
March 22, 2009

Hanging out with Milo at the guesthouse today, which means picture-palooza (cameras weren't allowed at the care center). Woot, woot.
March 23, 2009

Went out for pizza tonight in Ethiopia. Good to have a slice of home away from home.
March 23, 2009

Goodbye ceremony at the care center and made it through the embassy today. Milo is ours now and forever. Woot, woot.
March 24, 2009

Just sung Milo to sleep for the first time. My repertoire of U2 lullabies needs some work. It turned into one big medley.
March 24, 2009

Have I mentioned how cool it is that they serve Pepsi in glass bottles here in Ethiopia?
March 24, 2009

Last day in Ethiopia. Spent yesterday sick, so I'm hoping today goes better. Milo was sick last night, so I hope the flight home is OK.
March 26, 2009

Landed in DC. Can drink the tap water again. USA, USA!
March 27, 2009

Boarding plane for St. Paul. Woot, woot.
March 27, 2009

Touched down at MSP. Home.
March 27, 2009

Finally freaking home. About ready to collapse.
March 27, 2009

Milo is sleeping in a swing in the corner of my office. U2 is playing. Welcome home, kid. This is your universe.
March 28, 2009

Been home one day and more adoption paperwork arrived today. It truly doesn't end. But that's OK, I can put it off and play with Milo.
March 28, 2009

Lexi: "Twinkle, twinkle, little star ... Like a diamond where you live."
March 29, 2009

Fun evening: Abby was sick in bed while Milo spit up a half a bottle on me and Lexi was throwing a fit. Good thing my parents are here.
March 29, 2009

Third full day home and we wake up to Lexi throwing up. Lovely. Some day life will return to normal.
March 30, 2009

Welcome to Minnesota, Milo, it's snowing.
March 31, 2009

Chapter 4: Home

We no longer outnumber our children. This reality quickly set in.

Our flight arrived home Friday afternoon and that night was full of smiles and wonder and shell-shocked jetlag. I remember standing in the airport baggage claim watching as Lexi met Milo for the first time and I realizing I hadn't even acknowledged my parents yet, who were standing right next to us watching the entire scene. But by Saturday Abby was sick, Milo spat up entire bottles on me and Lexi kept throwing herself on the floor in colossal fits.

We now had to readjust to a larger, louder family. Many nights I'd sit there feeding Milo, soaking in the dueling feelings of exhaustion and relief. We were finally home, our journey to expand our family had finally happened. But now we had to settle into that reality.

Reality bites. Lexi loved her new little brother and relished her role as the big sister. She'd ask to hold Milo all the time and constantly showered him with love. But she also turned on us, going from pleasant to screaming and back again. And the precious child that barely made a noise in Ethiopia found his voice and let us know when hunger struck.

As we dealt with the exhaustion, relief and the return of "normal," Ethiopia always lingered in our thoughts. We will be forever connected with that land. I took countless blurry photos out the bus window trying to capture everything. But I'll never forget the moments: The bewildering first night when we were hustled by a man who wanted to carry our bags for a tip; the overwhelming and wonderful moment of meeting Milo for the first time; seeing street kids rocking Barack Obama T-shirts; glimpses of people huddled around muddy creeks, filling yellow cans with dirty water and hoisting them on their backs.

Ethiopia will always be in our hearts, and it was front and center in those days as we celebrated the minor accomplishments and reformed our family around this little wide-eyed wonder.

APRIL **2009**

Milo slept through the night last night for the first time. Yay for Milo! Yay for sleep!
April 2, 2009

Lexi just informed me that I can't call Milo a monkey because she's the monkey. Guess I need a new nickname.
April 3, 2009

Finally finished uploading all 1,200 pics from Ethiopia and our first day or so home with Milo. Whew.
April 3, 2009

My son's clothing informs me that he's "Dog gone cute," complete with a picture of a dog. Good thing—how else would I have known?
April 3, 2009

Milo's late afternoon scream-a-thons are not my favorite time of day.
April 6, 2009

Why does it always look like Milo is rubbing his hands together like a scheming mad scientist?
April 7, 2009

Bizarre evening: Taught Lexi how to sort playing cards by suit and then had a Homestar Runner style light switch rave with my Milo.
April 9, 2009

I love it! charity: water is drilling a well in Ethiopia this weekend. Clean water saves lives. Follow along and donate!
April 10, 2009

The Easter Sunday service is my favorite service of the year. Alleluia, Alleluia! Here's hoping Milo doesn't banish us to the cry room.
April 12, 2009

Not only did Milo banish me to the cry room, Lexi flung herself to the floor at the communion rail in a total fit. Go Easter.
April 12, 2009

And why did Lexi have a total fit in church? Because she couldn't kneel on the crouched sheep on the kneeler at the communion rail.
April 12, 2009

International clinic called this morning and apparently Milo has a parasitic stowaway, which explains why he spits up entire bottles. Fun.
April 13, 2009

Just watched video of American Internet geeks carrying 40 pounds of dirty water like Ethiopians do daily. Wow.
April 13, 2009

One of the parasites they mention in that video is the one Milo has. Imagine walking three hours for your daily water that makes you sick.
April 13, 2009

Abby's been gone with *both* kiddos since 11. What do I do? Catch up on work? Fold laundry? Take out trash? Clean kitchen? Home repair? Nap?
April 14, 2009

A day without shoes? TOMSshoes is challenging people to go barefoot on April 16 to raise awareness. Shoes (like water) can save lives.
April 14, 2009

What did I do while both kids were gone? Work, kitchen, trash and scraped paint. Then Milo came home and watched me scrape for half an hour.
April 14, 2009

We had a picnic supper at the park tonight. I went down the slide and fell on my ass. Lexi didn't catch me.
April 14, 2009

I just successfully put both kids to bed by myself (no thanks to the dogs), including a 45-minute screech-fest from Milo. I deserve snacks.
April 14, 2009

Lexi is having a complete meltdown. Why? We made her put pants on because the social worker is coming over. No secrets here.
April 15, 2009

In Ethiopia, approximately 1 million people suffer from a debilitating foot disease thanks to no shoes. Tomorrow is One Day Without Shoes.
April 15, 2009

Just wandered around home repair store with Milo sleeping in the sling. Nothing manlier than a sleeping baby in a hardware store.
April 15, 2009

Thinking about going shoeless tomorrow for Toms One Day Without Shoes. Wonder if U of MN doc's office will be a problem (i.e., shoes required?).
April 15, 2009

Maybe I should write a quirky grammar-spoofing guidebook: *Eats, Poops & Sleeps: The Zero Tolerance Approach to Parenting.*
April 16, 2009

Spent morning wandering around U of MN. Felt like freak with no shoes, baby in sling and taking pictures of art. What kind of campus hippie am I?
April 16, 2009

My feet are sore from walking around shoeless on smooth concrete and clean asphalt. How do real people do this every day? Eye-opening.
April 16, 2009

Me: "Lexi, did you hear the cow Milo was having when he didn't get his bottle?" Lexi: "Where is the cow?"
April 17, 2009

[Hopefully] taking the fam to see musician Shaun Groves tonight. Milo will likely sleep and Lexi wants to dance.

April 19, 2009

Saw Shaun Groves doing some acoustic rockin' tonight. Lexi danced, for about 10 minutes, then wandered the church. Milo mostly slept.

April 19, 2009

Abby: "Lexi, are you a little bit country or a little bit rock 'n roll?" Lexi: "I'm a little bit Lexi."

April 19, 2009

First step to surviving being double-teamed by your kids: Get up before them. Check. Second step: Watch them sleep in past 8. Um, check (weird).

April 20, 2009

Arg: Double-teamed! One child pees on bathroom rug while I give the other a bath. Wait, why would we put a bathroom rug under a potty-training child?

April 20, 2009

Obsessive photo parent failure: Lexi and I were both wearing our Red Wings jerseys on Saturday and I didn't get a picture of the two of us. Doh.

April 21, 2009

Milo and Lexi are squawking at each other. It's a cacophony of noise in my house. At least they're entertaining each other.

April 22, 2009

Today is about accomplishment: Painted doorframe, patched jeans, bathed baby, finished season 3 of *Lost*.

April 22, 2009

I love these exchanges. Lexi: "The pack 'n play is called a suitcase." Me: "No it's not, it's called a pack 'n play." Lexi: "Oh."

April 23, 2009

The bill came for Milo's 'welcome home' visit to the doctor: $2,600. I sure hope he gets on our insurance pretty soon.
April 23, 2009

- -

Milo polished off a whole container of baby applesauce. Score! First time he's done that for me. Today it's the small accomplishments.
April 23, 2009

- -

Both children are napping *at the same time!* [Kevin frantically rushes to get work done knowing wife won't be home until 8 tonight.]
April 23, 2009

- -

5:30 p.m. and Lexi says she wants to go to bed. Hmm... tempting. Very tempting.
April 23, 2009

- -

After getting spit up on one last time, both kids are in bed. I did all day solo. I don't know how single parents do it.
April 23, 2009

- -

Lexi is crying because I won't let her have ice cream for breakfast.
April 24, 2009

- -

So how's my day going? An hour ago, when my wife was supposed to be home, both kids were screaming and the dog was having a seizure. Fun.
April 24, 2009

- -

Milo just rolled over for the first time. Woohoo! (there's a milestone that's only exciting to parents)
April 27, 2009

- -

We take Milo to the doctor today. Bets on his current weight? April 8th he weighed 10.5 lbs. I'm betting 12.5 today.
April 27, 2009

- -

Uneventful doctor's visit for Milo, though he weighs in at a whopping 12 lbs., 8 oz. I called it. 2 lbs. in three weeks! Thanks for playing.
April 28, 2009

- -

OK Milo, 50% more bottle should mean 50% more nap, right? C'mon, work with me.

April 30, 2009

Lexi is running in circles with a pot on her head: "I'm a pothead!" Um, yeah.

April 30, 2009

MAY 2009

An old friend from high/middle school just found out they got their adoption referral. Woot, woot!

May 1, 2009

I feel like all I've accomplished this week is laundry and dishes. And the laundry isn't even folded yet.

May 1, 2009

Need patience I don't have with the children today. Lexi keeps asking pointless questions while Milo screams. Where's my sanity?

May 5, 2009

Milo asleep. Lexi "resting." Holing up in basement with lunch, *How I Met Your Mother* and lots of Pepsi and M&Ms. Need sanity.

May 5, 2009

OK, Milo, I know babies get messy when they eat. No big deal. But the bottom of your foot? Seriously?

May 6, 2009

Milo is now officially giardia-free. Woot, woot.

May 6, 2009

A sick Milo seems unable to sleep for more than 45 minutes a shot. It's going to be a long night.

May 6, 2009

Cut a sapling down yesterday and left it laying on the sidewalk cuz I'm lazy. Today Lexi had fun playing with it. Who needs toys?

May 8, 2009

Today should be fun. Ride the bus with two kids to get the car to take one of said kids to the doctor. Did I mention one is sick?

May 11, 2009

All that work to get to the doctor was worth it. Milo has pneumonia. Bleh. Now he gets meds, a nebulizer and a trip back to the doc tomorrow.

May 11, 2009

I'll say this for pneumonia: It means good, long naps. Milo's been sleeping well today. Hope that's true tonight as well.

May 11, 2009

CHAPTER 5: WATER

While "normalcy" (if you can call it that) settled in at home, I realized I had a heart to help. I would turn 30 in June and wanted to do something momentous to mark that milestone. But not for me.

When we were in Ethiopia bringing home Milo we witnessed the reality of unclean water:

- Time and time again we saw the people of Ethiopia carrying these five-gallon jerry cans, often walking hours to muddy holes for their daily supply of tainted water.

- Milo came home with giardia, a water-borne intestinal parasite common among people with no access to clean water.

- I fell sick for a day in Ethiopia, stricken down by water unintentionally consumed either in the shower or from rinsed dishes (thankfully it was a pretty mild case).

We knew firsthand the difference clean water could make. We also knew how easy it was to make a difference. Abby had been pushing charity: water since Christmas. For $20 they can provide one person with clean water for 20 years. So for my 30th birthday I decided to cash in my social networking chips and raise $600 to provide 30 people with clean water. I offered to shave my head if we could do it.

Little did I realize how woefully low I had set my expectations. In 30 days friends, family and total strangers donated $2,605 to celebrate my 30th birthday, giving clean water to 130 people. Best birthday ever.

And some people don't understand why I tweet.

There is an element of narcissism to social networking applications like Twitter or Facebook. But that's exactly why we need to look beyond ourselves. There are causes to be championed, daily lessons to be learned (Lexi constantly schools me in laughter and patience) and life to be shared. The choice between useless narcissism and world-changing optimism is up to you.

The Bald Birthday Benefit is coming. Hint: It involves water. (My attempt at an intriguing teaser. Be intrigued, it's been a long day.)
May 12, 2009

I turn 30 next month and it's going to be big. But not for me. Hopefully big for 30 other people. The Bald Birthday Benefit starts tomorrow.
May 14, 2009

Milo just shot me the pitiful 'Daddy, save me!' look while Abby started up the nebulizer. Sorry dude, it's for your own good.
May 14, 2009

I want to celebrate my 30th birthday with clean water for 30 people. If we do it I'll shave my head: Bald Birthday Benefit.
May 15, 2009

Life expectancy in Ethiopia: 45.5. United States: 77. Ouch. Clean water=life. $20 gives one person clean water for 20 years.
May 15, 2009

It's been 12 hours of the 30-day effort and the Bald Birthday Benefit is already at 20% of the goal. Wow. I am so bald.
May 15, 2009

42,000 people died last week from unsafe water and a lack of basic sanitation. 90% were children under 5. You can help: Donate to charity: water
May 17, 2009

Detroit comes home with the win. Awesome hockey. Spent the third period teaching Milo how to say, "SCORES!" We'll have to work on it.
May 17, 2009

I woke up this morning half bald! Metaphorically speaking of course. The Bald Birthday Benefit is over halfway. Give H2O.
May 18, 2009

These girls should be in school, but instead, they're hauling 40 pounds of water on their backs. You can help.
May 18, 2009

Lexi just asked, "Can I get my ballerina on?" As if prancing around the living room wasn't enough.
May 18, 2009

Watching Milo drop a rattle, roll over, pick it up and start shaking it again. He couldn't do that yesterday. Babies are crazy smart.
May 18, 2009

It's beautiful in Minnesota today. The sun is shining, the birds are singing, the kids are playing... and the teens are necking on the swings.
May 18, 2009

Just filled up the five-gallon jerry can on loan from charity: water to water the new hostas. Damn that's heavy.
May 18, 2009

Last night Milo loved his green beans. Today? Not so much. Then again, what did I expect? Who likes green beans for *breakfast*?
May 19, 2009

So Lexi can get up during her nap, fold her pants and put them away in the closet, but she can't get up to go poop in the toilet? Seriously?
May 19, 2009

Told Lexi about the Bald Birthday Benefit and shaving my head today. She asked if she could be bald. Um...
May 19, 2009

$20 can buy many peanuts, but it can also get me a haircut, a birthday present and one person clean water for 20 years.
May 20, 2009

Up at 5 a.m. feeding Milo. Apparently he woke the sun up too. Now Milo is fed, content and sleeping, but me and the sun can't go back to sleep. Doh.
May 20, 2009

Holy crap, I'm $60 away from being bald. Are we going to break the goal tonight? Give water.
May 20, 2009

More than 80% of Ethiopians lack clean water, according to SIM. Among worst in the world. You can help by donating to charity: water.
May 20, 2009

"It changed our lives forever." Read a great story about a family that adopted from Ethiopia and is now moving back.
May 20, 2009

Beautiful. Good news is a comin'! [Hint: Involves a shiny head]
May 21, 2009

You gave clean water to 30 people for my 30th birthday in just six days! Bald on June 13. Thanks. Now what? More water!
May 21, 2009

----

30 people will now get access to clean water. And in 23 days I'll shave my head. Thank you! (But it's not over)
May 21, 2009

Milo keeps sucking his toes. How is that fun? I mean, toe-jam. Ew.
May 21, 2009

Big, big thanks to everyone who has donated so far to make me bald and give life (water=life). Thank you.
May 21, 2009

Aw man, just got apple blueberry sauce on Milo's foot. That's not going to help with the toe sucking.
May 21, 2009

Quick 1.5-minute CNN video on charity: water and founder Scott Harrison: "I'm thankful every single day."
May 21, 2009

We hit $600 so on June 13 I'm bald, but who says we can't hit $5,000? Insane? Yes. So what? Now we're up to $640.
May 22, 2009

An old friend from BGEA days is raising money to pay for final expenses of a *third* adoption. $25 gets you a T-shirt.
May 22, 2009

Love today's pic of the day from charity: water. Woman in Ethiopia tossing popcorn in the air to celebrate water.
May 22, 2009

Many people in the developing world walk more than three hours daily for clean water. I walk, um, 10 feet? Give water.
May 22, 2009

Just walked to the Mississippi and back (four miles total) to get a sense of what many people have to do for water.
May 22, 2009

4,500 kids will die today because they lack clean water. That's dumb. $20 gives them water. Save a life.
May 26, 2009

Lexi and Milo shared a room for the first time last night. Went great. Lexi even put a blanket back on Milo at some point in the night.
May 26, 2009

$835 raised so far for the Bald Birthday Benefit. That means 41 people get clean water and come June 13 I'm bald. Thanks!
May 26, 2009

This morning Lexi went from comatose to spaz in under 15 minutes.
May 27, 2009

I credit my wife and Milo for waking me up to the issue of water. Experiencing it firsthand is pretty eye opening.
May 27, 2009

My dog Speak is smart enough not to bite Milo when he grabs chunks of Speak's fur, but not smart enough to walk away.
May 27, 2009

A crowd of kids throwing their arms in the air for water. This is how I want to celebrate my 30th birthday.
May 28, 2009

Milo is rolling across the room, ready to take this weekend by force.
May 29, 2009

This morning Lexi is singing the "No More Monkeys Jumping on the Bed" song: "No more junkies, monkeying on the bed!"
May 30, 2009

Watched *Lilo & Stitch* tonight with Lexi. Don't remember tearing up last time I saw it. "It's my family. Is small and broken, but still good."
May 30, 2009

Just got a reminder to wear the traditional red to Pentecost Sunday at church tomorrow. My Red Wings jersey is red.
May 31, 2009

JUNE 2009

Hey, it's June! Only 13 days until I shave my head. Clean shave=clean water. We can still add to the total.
June 1, 2009

Off to the doctor this morning. Bets on how much Milo weighs? I'm guessing 15 pounds.

June 2, 2009

Milo weighs in at 14.5 lbs. Doc said: "He has had *amazing* growth within the last month." Woot, woot.

June 2, 2009

Lexi: "I want to carry water. But I need help." From the mouths of babes (whose dad talks about it all the time).

June 2, 2009

Last day with kids before wife home for summer not going well. Lexi in her room with no lunch (her choice) and toy shelves bare, thanks to bad choices.

June 3, 2009

On the plus side, Milo—or 2 a.m. boy, as I like to call him—has been sound asleep for two hours.

June 3, 2009

I'm looking forward to being old and senile so I can return the favor and scream at my kids and then throw up on them.

June 3, 2009

Two a.m. boy struck again. Blast.

June 4, 2009

Want to improve your self-esteem? Take a 3-year-old clothes shopping. Lexi: "Mama, you're beautiful."

June 4, 2009

On Sunday I'm going to walk two miles carrying five gallons of water to see what life is like for the 1 billion without water.

June 5, 2009

Lexi is finally realizing how many of her toys were taken away the other day because she wouldn't clean up. Ah, sweet justice.

June 5, 2009

Just got off the phone with the *Pioneer Press* for my Walk for Water deal. Might be in tomorrow's paper. Cool!

June 5, 2009

I've got tears in my eyes thanks to charity: water's Born in September campaign. Looks like water for birthdays is catching on.

June 5, 2009

Maza Hapes wakes up at 4 a.m., waits 1.5 hours for her turn to get water in Ethiopia. She washes kids once every three weeks.

June 5, 2009

The *Pioneer Press* did a brief write-up on my Walk for Water effort.

June 6, 2009

Of course I won dumb quote of the year award: "Lugging 40 pounds of water 'will actually be fairly strenuous' he said."

June 6, 2009

Ha! A friend from church saw the *Pioneer Press* article on my Walk for Water and wants to come with me tomorrow. Cool.

June 6, 2009

Today's the day: Carrying five gallons of water two miles. Water=life.

June 7, 2009

I made it. Five gallons (40 pounds). Two miles. Wow. Some people do that every day. Crazy. Give water.

June 7, 2009

When Lexi saw me coming: "There's my daddy with the gross water."

June 7, 2009

After carrying five gallons of water (40 pounds) two miles yesterday, it's safe to say I'm "fairly" sore today.
June 8, 2009

According to Lexi, Milo isn't ours, he's the church's. ("It's the church's" is what Lexi says when she thinks you need to share)
June 9, 2009

You've given $1,910 so far—clean water for 95 people! Five days to go. Thank you.
June 9, 2009

Dear Children, you're not cute when one barfs in the crib and the other pees on the couch. Especially during playoff hockey.
June 9, 2009

Every time I get up I'm reminded about Sunday's walk. "Fairly" sore indeed. Somebody tell me to shut up and quit my whining.
June 9, 2009

The iPhone has nothing on Lexi. She just used a Cheerio phone. Yes, that's a phone made out of breakfast cereal. She talked to Mom and Milo.
June 10, 2009

There's lots of giggling coming from Lexi and Milo's room. Hmm... investigate? Or be glad it's not screaming? Going with ignorance is bliss.
June 12, 2009

Lexi is leaving the house in her ballerina slippers. At least it's not the full outfit, right?
June 12, 2009

Can shaken baby syndrome be self-inflicted? Milo's kind of wild. Just wondering.
June 12, 2009

So far you've given clean water to 114 people. Crazy! Tomorrow I shave my head and stick a fork in the Bald Birthday Benefit.
June 12, 2009

OK, Milo, here's the deal: You woke up during the first period of Stanley Cup hockey. You must sleep through all subsequent periods. Deal?
June 12, 2009

Lexi: "Mommy, I think Milo hit me in the face!" He's only 8 months old and she's already tattling on what could be construed as hitting.
June 13, 2009

Today's the last day for the Bald Birthday Benefit. Wish me a happy birthday with clean water. Tonight I shave my head.
June 13, 2009

I just brushed Mazie in the backyard. Our lawn is now the color of dog. Better than the carpet I guess.
June 13, 2009

Brushed shedding dog outside, vacuumed inside and now there's a Mazie-shaped ball of fur on the carpet. "Mazie? Did you sit down?" Doh.
June 13, 2009

It's head shaving time
June 13, 2009

And... I'm bald.
June 13, 2009

Celebrating my 30th birthday with baldness and clean water for 130 people. Thank you.
June 13, 2009

Huh. Feels a little... drafty this morning.
June 14, 2009

Lexi: "I like your new head."
June 14, 2009

It cracks me up when babies can only roll over in one direction. Milo is getting mad right now because he can't roll the other way.

June 15, 2009

Thank you hardly begins to cover my gratitude for the clean water given to 130 people, but thank you.

June 15, 2009

Off to renew my driver's license and immortalize my bald head until the next renewal.

June 15, 2009

To anyone jealous that I still have this much hair to shave, I saw a lot of gray when it came off. There's a silver fox in my future.

June 15, 2009

CHAPTER 6: FAMILY

Life goes on. The highs and low of our adoption process begin to fade away in the everyday routine of bibs, baths and bedtimes. I still juggle work and the kids, often with less patience and grace than I care to admit.

If I've learned anything in this process it's that life goes on. The responsibilities, bills and deadlines will always be there, coming and going, never ceasing. The laundry and dishes are never done. But every day there are opportunities to laugh and moments to make a difference. An enormous step like adoption really isn't one big step, it's a thousand little ones made by a thousand people. It's the slow drip of progress that changes the world. And we can't do it alone.

That's why there's no Hollywood ending to this story. Life goes on. Lexi will keep on saying and doing hilarious things. Milo will catch up to his big sister and let his voice be heard. Deadlines and projects will come and go. Mazie will surely eat something she's not supposed to. Adoption and Ethiopia and causes like water will always be important to us.

I'm sure another technological wonder will replace Twitter and make this seem so archaic, but it doesn't matter. We'll still find a way to connect with one another, share our hopes and dreams, our laughter and tears. Technology will continue to advance and make each bewildered generation the butt of the next generation's jokes. But people are still people. We still love, we still care, we still hope. Some days we just need a little perspective. A little reminder that life is wonderful and funny and— dammit, Milo's playing in the toilet.

Life goes on.

Being responsible and skipping zoo trip today to get work done. Being responsible sucks.

June 19, 2009

Just caught Lexi standing in Milo's crib during "nap" time. Sigh.

June 19, 2009

Just took an electrical cord away from Milo. I'm such a mean parent.

June 20, 2009

It's so humid today our wall of Christmas cards on the cupboard is falling down. Maybe that's a sign.

June 22, 2009

The dog fell off the couch tonight. Hilarious.

June 22, 2009

Benefit of adoption: Eye doctor said Milo will *never* need glasses. I bet that's not true for Lexi.

June 23, 2009

Abby: "Hey Lexi, we got you a new carseat." Lexi: "Oh, and a new car, too?" Um, nice try, kid.

June 23, 2009

Getting up at 5 a.m. with the kid? That's OK. Getting up at 5 a.m. with the dog? Because he's scared of a thunderstorm? Not OK.

June 25, 2009

TV: "You're a super-reader!" Lexi (to the TV): "I'm not super-reader. I'm Lexi."

June 26, 2009

That's the benefit of children. I just ask Lexi to draw a picture and then write Happy _____ across the top. Hallmark is trembling.

June 27, 2009

At TGI Friday's last night Lexi started singing "Maniac" from *Flashdance*. Had an entire table laughing. "She's a maniac, maniac..."
June 27, 2009

Not only is Lexi singing the 80s, but Abby is tie-dyeing. I think I've fallen into a time warp. Need neon yellow clothing.
June 27, 2009

TCF Bank's list of occupations includes pawnbroker but not writer or editor. Ouch.
June 29, 2009

Grappling with the idea that pawnbroker is a more ubiquitous occupation than writer (according to my bank) and what that means for society.
June 29, 2009

JULY 2009

I'm not sure if Milo realizes that it's possible to communicate in something other than high-pitched tones.
July 3, 2009

Abby and Lexi are watching *Saved by the Bell*. The early (middle school) years. Yikes.
July 4, 2009

Lexi's eating a full-size carrot and I'm teaching her to say, "What's up Doc?" She has no idea what it's referring to.
July 4, 2009

Fourth of July sucks. The dogs are freaked out and Milo is screaming bloody murder. Who says fireworks are fun?
July 4, 2009

I can hear Milo through the window. He's making noise and could easily be mistaken for a honking goose.
July 6, 2009

Imagine not calling your child by name for fear they won't live. Heartbreaking poverty needs action.

July 13, 2009

Photo of the Day from charity: water—celebration of a new well in Southern Ethiopia (Milo is from Southern Ethiopia).

July 17, 2009

Gave Lexi a high five today for not peeing in her underwear during naptime. Some days I think my standards are low.

July 19, 2009

Milo keeps screaming tonight, prompting Lexi to issue an ultimatum: "Either give him a bottle or put him upstairs." They share a room.

July 19, 2009

11-year-old sells toys to help family: "You can't live in toys or eat toys. Even though they are fun, you don't need them."

July 20, 2009

Milo kicks like a maniac. We could hook him up to a generator and power something. How cool would Milo-powered lights be?

July 20, 2009

Lexi screams: "I'll be good!" Nice try. Actions speak louder than words. OK, your words are technically louder, but that's not the point.

July 21, 2009

I shaved my head about a month ago and it's already starting to stick up in back. The other day Lexi called it my "baby hair."

July 21, 2009

Milo's shirt says "I love dad." Rock on. But it's a hand-me-down. So does the love apply to original Dad or hand-me-down Dad?

July 23, 2009

Lexi: "What's Milo eating?" Abby: "Sweet potatoes." Lexi: "I don't like that." Abby: "Well, you don't have to eat it." Lexi: "Can I try it?"
July 24, 2009

Dogs are now realizing the wonderful potential of Milo. He's started eating those baby puffs and drops them everywhere.
July 24, 2009

Lexi: "I'm a kind of a little bit starving, I think."
July 26, 2009

Me: "I need to go upstairs and change." Lexi: "OK, let's go upstairs and change Daddy." Uh... no thanks?
July 26, 2009

I just scolded Lexi for yelling at Milo. Her defense: "Milo was looking at me!"
July 27, 2009

I just exacted the Daddy Tax on Lexi's ice cream. Score!
July 28, 2009

AUGUST 2009

Took a tour of Yale today. Lexi asked if she could eat the grapes and pointed at the acorns on the ground. Guess none of the smart rubbed off.
August 3, 2009

Me: "Nobody wants your bare butt on the couch!" Lexi: "Bear? I'm not a bear!"
August 5, 2009

Took Lexi to the M&M store in Times Square. She ignored wall-to-wall pick-a-color M&Ms in favor of the 8 oz. pack you can get at any gas station in the country.
August 7, 2009

Score. Wife is picking up Dairy Queen on the way home. Always makes up for dealing with crabby children.
August 10, 2009

Woke up to discover a bucket on Milo's head. Ah, the hazards of making your children share a room.
August 11, 2009

Me: "Lexi, how much pasta do you want?" Lexi: "5 years old!" Me: [puzzled look]
August 11, 2009

Lexi: "I scooted all the way back on the toilet!" Me: "That's great, Lex." Lexi: "Yeah, it was amazing."
August 12, 2009

Lexi: "Do you want to sing rock-a-bye or ABCs?" Abby: "Rock-a-bye." Lexi: "No, the rock-a-bye is silly. How about ABCs?"
August 13, 2009

Lexi is playing her xylophone and taking requests: "Do you want to hear the fish song or the hurt has an owie?"
August 13, 2009

Just took down all the Christmas cards displayed on our cupboard. It was time.
August 15, 2009

Lunch with musician Justin McRoberts. Lexi didn't want to go home: "But I want him to give me a hug!" I think someone has a new fan.
August 16, 2009

Wife went back to school today. Just like that, summer's over. I think I'm in mourning.
August 17, 2009

Lexi: "My crayon broke. I have to go home."
August 17, 2009

In rural Ethiopia, 40% of men do not live to celebrate their 40th birthday. That changes now, for Milo and so many others.
August 17, 2009

Lexi: "Ring around the rosie, actions, actions, we all fall down!"
August 17, 2009

We have forward progress! Milo just crawled across the kitchen floor.
August 17, 2009

During our vacation a third party confirmed that Milo's babbling is coherent. His first official words: "Mama" and "Dada." I'm officially proud.
August 17, 2009

By the way, Lexi's first word? "Hi."
August 17, 2009

Just realized Milo's toddler toothpaste is funny because it says "Training Toothpaste" and has a picture of a train on it!
August 18, 2009

Milo refused to take a nap this evening, so he got to mow the lawn on my back. Yet another benefit of a rotary mower: quiet enough for baby.
August 18, 2009

Lexi came home from the store wearing her new shoes. Now she wants to wear them to bed.
August 18, 2009

Abby: "Lexi, bedtime!" (after the fourth stalling tactic) Lexi: "Sometimes you have to wait patiently."
August 18, 2009

Milo just crawled out of sight in the kitchen. Realize I need to start closing the baby gate. Wow. Mobile baby happens so quickly.
August 19, 2009

Lexi refuses to go to her room and get dressed because "there's a big scary Lexi down there!"

August 21, 2009

Lexi: "Don't throw Milo." Me: "Why not?" Lexi: "He's not a ball." Words of wisdom.

August 24, 2009

Lexi: "My fingernails are getting long. They're making me dangerous."

August 24, 2009

Lexi just tried to convince me that she was wearing pants-underwear, not just underwear, and could therefore go outside.

August 24, 2009

Lexi wants a haircut and we're discussing how short. Lexi: "Daddy, I can't shave my head, I'm a girl! You shave your head!"

August 25, 2009

Lexi is off to get a haircut because she doesn't like ponytails.

August 25, 2009

In the interest of sibling equality, I just posted a cute video of Milo crawling. We had better video, but Lexi walked into it pantsless.

August 26, 2009

Now I know why there are always fewer pics of second child—the first child ruins all the photo opps.

August 26, 2009

OK, Milo. Incessant screaming can now turn into incessant napping. Please? Thanks.

August 26, 2009

Taking Lexi and Milo to the Social Media Breakfast at the Minnesota State Fair tomorrow. Hoping Lexi will help me tag team on the networking. She's my helper monkey.
August 27, 2009

Survived about six hours of Minnesota State Fair with Lexi and Milo by myself. Everyone fell asleep on the way home. Well, almost everyone.
August 28, 2009

Wearing hoodies in Minnesota.
August 29, 2009

I can read *Where the Wild Things Are* to Lexi because "it's not scary at all," but I have to put it away in the playroom so it doesn't scare her.
August 31, 2009

SEPTEMBER 2009

Lexi is watching *The Incredibles*: "But 'Mr. Incrapable' is not scary."
September 1, 2009

It's not a real home repair project until you draw blood. Uh, check.
September 2, 2009

Lexi: "I want something else to eat." Me: "OK, what do you want?" Lexi: "Meat!" Me: "Meat?! What kind of meat?" Lexi: "Green meat!"
September 2, 2009

Lexi: "Oh, Dad, you're such a boy sometimes." Me: "I am?" Lexi: "Yeah, see your head? It's a boy right there."
September 3, 3009

Milo has reached that point of babyhood where Cheerios can now be found where you least expect them. Like in his diaper.
September 3, 2009

Lexi, on not finishing her orange juice with pulp: "I don't like the 'plope.' It's not my favorite."
September 4, 2009

Lexi would like you to know that her Frisbee and her flavor ice match. They're both red.
September 4, 2009

Naptime ended early. Kids are turning my office into a playground. Milo is intently crawling towards my router and Lexi is throwing things.
September 4, 2009

Lexi to me: "Mama said we're going out to eat." Lexi to Mama: "Daddy said we can go out to eat." We just got played by a 3-year-old.
September 4, 2009

Lexi: "I have to pack up my lunch." Puts a baby in her lunch box.
September 8, 2009

What we learned from Lexi tonight: You wear a seatbelt on the airplane so you don't fall out and get an owie.
September 8, 2009

Lexi after watching *Clifford the Big Red Dog*: "Why is Clifford big?" You know, that's a good question. Growth hormones? Mutant? Government experiment?
September 9, 2009

Milo figured out his roll around toy, but he keeps watching me smile rather than watch to see where his ball comes out.
September 9, 2009

Lexi: "Oh no! Milo's playing with the trashcan. What are we going to do?" We're going to hope he takes it out. Tomorrow's trash day.
September 10, 2009

Today's the Ethiopian New Year (long story, but they use a different calendar—it's 2002). Here's to new beginnings for Africa and her people.
September 11, 2009

Horrible news about stolen children for adoption in Guatemala (from 1977-1989). This is why the red tape exists.
September 12, 2009

Explaining a broadcast TV schedule in an on-demand era is just ridiculous. Sorry Lexi, but *Sesame Street* isn't on yet and I can't change it.
September 14, 2009

I think I lack sympathy. Lexi: "Dad, there's a big scary monster down here!" Me: "That's OK. Tell him I said hi."
September 15, 2009

Milo's new favorite game? Closing the door and shutting himself into the bathroom, playroom or wherever he is, then pretending he's a doorstop
September 15, 2009

We just got more stuff notarized for Milo last night. It never ends! But it is so worth it.
September 19, 2009

Ah, buckling down for a couple hours of productivity at 6 p.m. on a Saturday night. Yes, the life of a work-at-home dad is glamorous.
September 19, 2009

Me: "Lexi, those socks don't even match." Lexi: "Matching socks?! No way!"
September 21, 2009

Writing yet another adoption check for Milo. This time it's a filing fee to finalize the adoption in the U.S. Final is good. I like that.
September 21, 2009

Milo's complete inability to fall asleep on his own is damaging my calm.
September 23, 2009

Ah. Milo finally asleep. I think I nearly came unhinged. May need to call in reinforcements if he keeps this up.

September 23, 2009

10:30 and we're fighting to get Milo to sleep. I guess better now than 2 a.m. Good thing I called a babysitter for tomorrow.

September 23, 2009

This morning Milo rolled off the changing table and I showed athletic prowess I know I don't have by catching him before he hit the floor.

September 24, 2009

"Say cheese!" This morning Lexi took my picture using a piece of toast.

September 24, 2009

Me: [Singing the breakfast time song to Milo.] Lexi: "Daddy, you're just a silly boy, aren't you?"

September 29, 2009

I hope Milo will forgive me for mixing banana raspberry oatmeal with mixed veggies and beef, but it's the only way he'll eat the veggies and beef.

September 29, 2009

Off to the post office to re-mail adoption docs. Apparently we were supposed to actually sign the documents. Oops.

September 29, 2009

Lexi: "Who's that in the picture taking care of Milo?" Me: "A nanny in Ethiopia before Milo came to stay with us." Lexi: "He's my favorite kid."

September 29, 2009

Tonight I caught myself shouting Lexi's full name when she was in trouble. For future reference: Not very effective and sounds ridiculous.

September 29, 2009

Me: "Lexi, Milo's head is not a drum!" Lexi: "It's not? Then what is it?" Me: "It's a … um… it's a head—just stop drumming it!"
September 30, 2009

OCTOBER 2009

I don't know how, but Milo managed to get baby food up my sleeve—all the way to my elbow. Ew.
October 1, 2009

As a work-at-home dad, some days I really envy the ability others have to go out at night and be social. Not that I was ever social.
October 1, 2009

No power for a couple hours this morning. Had to actually clean off my desk in order to maintain productivity.
October 5, 2009

Milo is playing with Mazie's dog bone. Normally I'd take it away, but it's the first time he's stopped screaming. I'm going with it.
October 5, 2009

Lexi trying to get Milo to say 'Mama' is cute. But not at 4:30 in the morning. Nothing is cute at 4:30 in the morning. No, not even puppies.
October 6, 2009

Lexi, looking at me over her sunglasses: "I have to go." Me: "Did you finish your cereal?" Lexi, pushing glasses back up: "I have to go."
October 6, 2009

Feeding Milo is now an act of performance art. Weird noises and faces seem like a fair trade for a spoonful of sludge.
October 6, 2009

I don't know how people maintain patience in the face of screaming children. Let's face it: I suck at it.

October 6, 2009

Walk out of Milo's line of sight for two seconds and he screams. Bash his head on a doorframe and he shrugs. Babies are weird.

October 6, 2009

Lexi: "I'm NOT a crabasaur!" Me: "Yes you are." Lexi: "NO I'M NOT!"

October 7, 2009

In the U.S. there are 100,000 children awaiting adoption and 300,000 churches. You do the math.

October 9, 2009

Lexi, pushing Milo on the riding toy: "You want to go for a ride, Milo? Hold on, I have to get all the crap out of the way."

October 9, 2009

Lexi: "You have to be 18 years old to read a monster book."

October 12, 2009

We go to court next week to finalize Milo's adoption! That means birth certificate, official name change, etc. A formality, but exciting.

October 12, 2009

I'm going to be homeless, again. I'm sleeping outside on Thursday to raise money for local homeless shelters. Want to donate?

October 12, 2009

On Thursday I'm going to sleep outside to help the homeless. Today it's snowing. Doh.

October 12, 2009

Abby: "You need to listen or I'll pick the movie and it'll be a boring movie!" Lexi: "What kind of boring movie?"

October 13, 2009

Love seeing the images of Ethiopians getting clean water. Go charity: water!
October 13, 2009

I'm sleeping outside tonight to support the homeless, rain or shine. Uh, what about snow? Ha! I prefer snow to rain.
October 15, 2009

Let's see: Overnight low of 35, 30-40% chance of precipitation (snow/rain). Being homeless sucks. And I'm only doing it one night.
October 15, 2009

Lexi: "Is *Sesame Street* on yet?" Me: "Not yet. You know, you could skip it once in a while." Lexi: "I don't know, Dad..."
October 15, 2009

Checking the forecast one more time before getting dressed. Yep—cold tonight. How do people who are actually homeless do it?
October 15, 2009

After a night out I get to come home and it's all back to normal. Real homeless do it day in, day out. That's got to be crushing—can't imagine.
October 16, 2009

Youngest person in a Project Home shelter last night was three months old. As InvisiblePeople.tv founder Mark Horvath says, kids shouldn't be homeless. Amen.
October 16, 2009

Celebrated Milo's birthday tonight. He liked the cupcakes and wrapping paper.
October 18, 2009

50% of all schools in the world don't have clean water. How dumb is that?
October 20, 2009

I know I'm a dad because I walk around and shut off the lights.
October 21, 2009

Tomorrow is Milo's big day in court. More of a formality and should be fun, but it feels big and intimidating.

October 21, 2009

Back from the courthouse. Milo's a citizen. We're official. Lexi: "We're a family!"

October 22, 2009

I just walked around the corner to see Lexi playing with the iPod Touch. How long until she's tweeting the funny/stupid things I do/say?

October 25, 2009

THE END

HELPING THE CAUSE

A portion of the proceeds from this book will go to charity: water to fund a well in Ethiopia. It will take $5,000 to build a well in Ethiopia. That's a lot of books. If you'd like to make an additional donation or learn more about adoption, Twitter, Ethiopia, charity: water or any of the other topics and organizations mentioned in this book, please visit:

KevinDHendricks.com/books/adoption

Many thanks...

Josh Lewis for turning me on to Twitter. I suppose I have him to blame/thank for many of my tech addictions.

Abby, Lexi and Milo for being the family.

Tim, Nicole and Abby for giving early feedback and editing help. Brian White for the design work and Ronald Cox for the layout. The many people who have turned me on to causes and the need for justice and compassion in our world, especially Jody Landers with Water for Christmas and Scott Harrison and the charity: water team.

The many people who responded to my tweets about Lexi, both on Twitter and Facebook, who encouraged me to keep on sharing the goofy things Lexi says and does.

Children's Home Society and Family Services both in Minnesota and Ethiopia, the group of fellow adoptive parents we traveled with, and the many people who supported our adoption.

Photos: BarbaraOBrienPhoto.com & Kevin D. Hendricks.

ABOUT THE AUTHOR

Kevin D. Hendricks lives in St. Paul, Minn., with his wife, two kids and two dogs. He runs his own freelance writing and editing company, Monkey Outta Nowhere. He's delved into the printed word before with several book projects and more in the works. You can learn more at KevinDHendricks.com, which is also where you'll find the blog he's updated since 1998. For shorter bursts of narcissism you can follow him at Twitter.com/KevinHendricks.

www.ingramcontent.com/pod-product-compliance
Lightning Source LLC
Chambersburg PA
CBHW061025050326
40689CB00012B/2701